~A BINGO BOOK~

The Middle Ages Bingo Book

COMPLETE BINGO GAME IN A BOOK

I0167325

Written By Rebecca Stark

Educational Books 'n' Bingo

ADDITION BINGO DIRECTIONS

INCLUDED:

List of Terms

Templates for Additional Terms and Clues

2 Clues per Term

30 Unique Bingo Cards

Markers

1. **Either cut apart the book or make copies of ALL the sheets. You might want to make an extra copy of the clue sheets to use for introduction and review. Keep the sheets in an envelope for easy reuse.**

2. Cut apart the call cards with terms and clues.

3. Pass out one bingo card per student. There are enough for a class of 30.

4. Pass out markers. You may cut apart the markers included in this book or use any other small items of your choice.

5. Decide whether or not you will require the entire card to be filled. Requiring the entire card to be filled provides a better review. However, if you have a short time to fill, you may prefer to have them do the just the border or some other format. Tell the class before you begin what is required.

6. There are 50 terms. Read the list before you begin. If there are any terms that have not been covered in class, you may want to read to the students the term and clues before you begin.

7. There is a blank space in the middle of each card. You can instruct the students to use it as a free space or you can write in answers to cover terms not included. Of course, in this case you would create your own clues. (Templates provided.)

8. Shuffle the cards and place them in a pile. Two or three clues are provided for each term. If you plan to play the game with the same group more than once, you might want to choose a different clue for each game. If not, you may choose to use more than one clue.

9. Be sure to keep the cards you have used for the present game in a separate pile. When a student calls, "Bingo," he or she will have to verify that the correct answers are on his or her card AND that the markers were placed in response to the proper questions. Pull out the cards that are on the student's card keeping them in the order they were used in the game. Read each clue as it was given and ask the student to identify the correct answer from his or her card.

10. If the student has the correct answers on the card AND has shown that they were marked in response to the *correct questions,* then that student is the winner and the game is over. If the student does not have the correct answers on the card OR he or she marked the answers in response to *the wrong questions,* then the game continues until there is a proper winner.

11. If you want to play again, reshuffle the cards and begin again.

Have fun!

ADDITION BINGO DIRECTIONS

INCLUDED:

List of Terms

Templates for Additional Terms and Clues

2 Clues per Term

30 Unique Bingo Cards

Markers

1. **Either cut apart the book or make copies of ALL the sheets. You might want to make an extra copy of the clue sheets to use for introduction and review. Keep the sheets in an envelope for easy reuse.**

2. Cut apart the call cards with terms and clues.

3. Pass out one bingo card per student. There are enough for a class of 30.

4. Pass out markers. You may cut apart the markers included in this book or use any other small items of your choice.

5. Decide whether or not you will require the entire card to be filled. Requiring the entire card to be filled provides a better review. However, if you have a short time to fill, you may prefer to have them do the just the border or some other format. Tell the class before you begin what is required.

6. There are 50 terms. Read the list before you begin. If there are any terms that have not been covered in class, you may want to read to the students the term and clues before you begin.

7. There is a blank space in the middle of each card. You can instruct the students to use it as a free space or you can write in answers to cover terms not included. Of course, in this case you would create your own clues. (Templates provided.)

8. Shuffle the cards and place them in a pile. Two or three clues are provided for each term. If you plan to play the game with the same group more than once, you might want to choose a different clue for each game. If not, you may choose to use more than one clue.

9. Be sure to keep the cards you have used for the present game in a separate pile. When a student calls, "Bingo," he or she will have to verify that the correct answers are on his or her card AND that the markers were placed in response to the proper questions. Pull out the cards that are on the student's card keeping them in the order they were used in the game. Read each clue as it was given and ask the student to identify the correct answer from his or her card.

10. If the student has the correct answers on the card AND has shown that they were marked in response to the *correct questions,* then that student is the winner and the game is over. If the student does not have the correct answers on the card OR he or she marked the answers in response to *the wrong questions,* then the game continues until there is a proper winner.

11. If you want to play again, reshuffle the cards and begin again.

Have fun!

TERMS

BATTLE OF HASTINGS

THE BLACK DEATH

CASTLES

CATHEDRALS

CHANSONS DE GESTE

CHARLEMAGNE

CHARTRES

GEOFFREY CHAUCER

CHIVALRY

CHRÉTIEN DE TROYES

THE CHURCH

EL CID

CHRISTOPHER COLUMBUS

COPERNICUS

CRAFTSMEN

THE CRUSADES

DANTE ALIGHIERI

THE DARK AGES

ELEANOR OF AQUITAINE

LEIF ERIKSON

FABLES

FAIRS

THE FEUDAL SYSTEM

SAINT FRANCIS OF ASSISI

GOTHIC ARCHITECTURE

JOHANNES GUTENBERG

HERALDIC DEVICES

JOAN OF ARC

KING ARTHUR

KNIGHTS

LEONARDO DA VINCI

FERDINAND MAGELLAN

THE MAGNA CARTA

MARCO POLO

MERCHANTS

MICHELANGELO

THE MIDDLE AGES

MONKS

THE MOORS

PEASANTS

THE RENAISSANCE

RICHARD I

SALADIN

SUITS OF ARMOR

THOMAS À BECKET

TOURNAMENTS

TRIAL BY ORDEAL

POPE URBAN II

THE VIKINGS

WILLIAM THE CONQUEROR

Additional Terms

Choose as many additional topics as you would like and write them in the squares. Repeat each as desired.
Cut out the squares and randomly distribute them to the class.
Instruct the students to place their square on the center space of their card.

The Middle Ages Bingo

Clues for Additional Terms

Write three clues for each of your additional terms.
Make copies of this template as needed.

_____	_____
1.	1.
2.	2.
3.	3.
_____	_____
1.	1.
2.	2.
3.	3.
_____	_____
1.	1.
2.	2.
3.	3.

© Barbara M. Peller

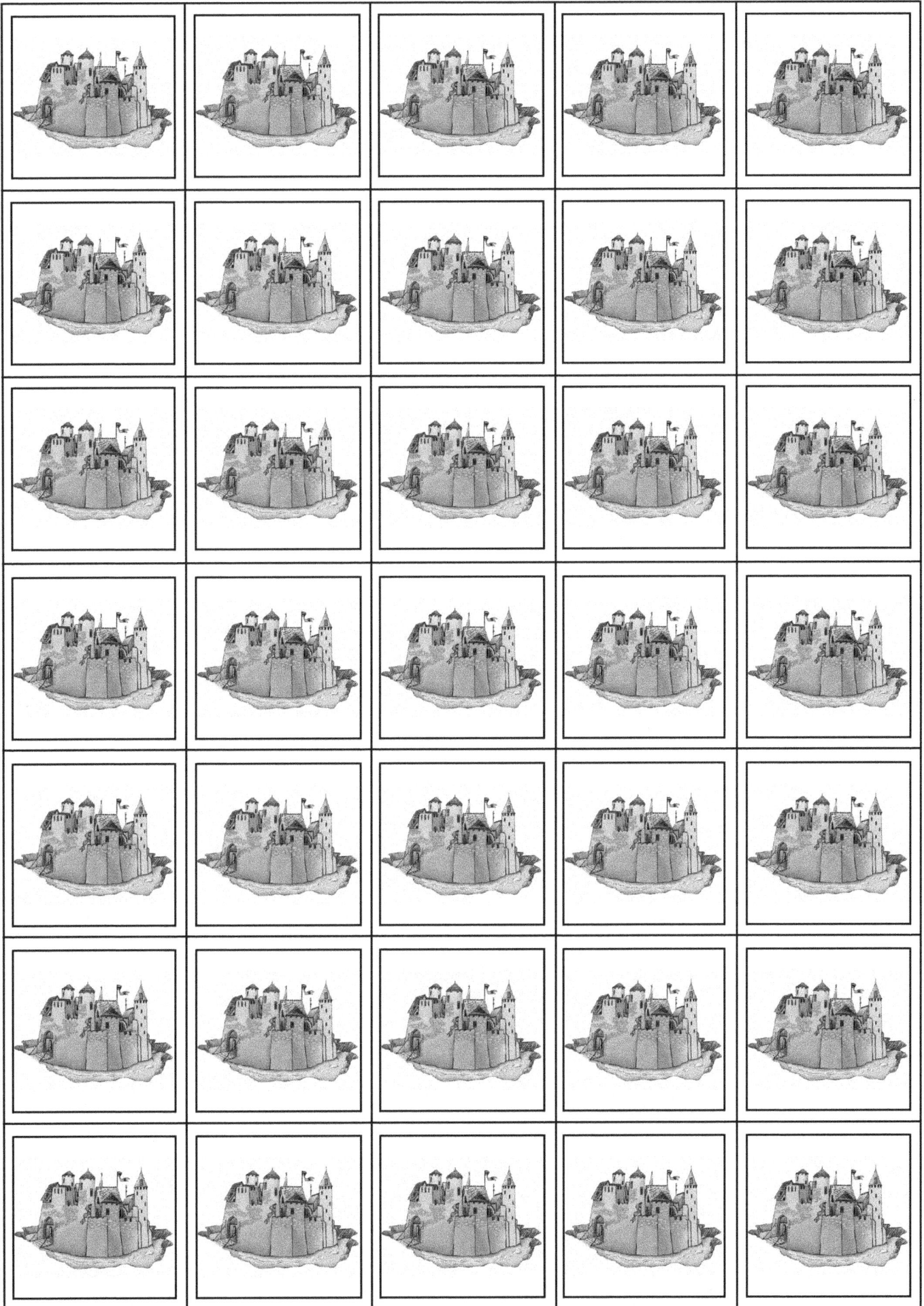

PEASANTS	THE MIDDLE AGES
1. This class worked the land and produced the goods that the lord and his manor needed. 2. They were heavily taxed and were required to relinquish much of what they harvested. They did not even "belong to" themselves according to medieval law. 3. Semi-free ones worked the lord's demesne and paid him dues in return for the use of land.	1. Typically, the period stretches from the collapse of Imperial Rome to the coming together of the forces of the Renaissance in Europe. 2. It is another name for the Medieval Era. 3. The intelligentsia of the Renaissance labeled the years preceding their own as this.
CHARTRES	**DANTE ALIGHIERI**
1. In the 12th century, a cathedral was built in this town southwest of Paris. 2. The 12-century cathedral there is a symbol of the importance of religion in the Middle Ages. 3. A communal enterprise designed and executed the cathedral here.	1. Exile from Florence gave this writer time to create *The Divine Comedy.* 2. His *The Divine Comedy* was an epic account of the poet's journey through purgatory and hell to heaven. 3. In his *The Inferno,* the poet encountered those who in his view sinned on Earth—politicians, liars, murderers, etc.
LEIF ERIKSON	**THE VIKINGS**
1. This Norse explorer was probably the first European to have landed in North America. 2. It is believed that he was born about 970 CE in Iceland. 3. He went to Norway to serve the King of Norway, Olaf I. When he returned to Greenland, he explored the land west of Greenland, likely Newfoundland, Canada.	1.These Norse seafaring warriors and traders originated in Scandinavia and raided the coasts of Britain, Ireland and mainland Europe from the late 8th to the 11th century. 2. In addition to the warriors and traders, the term denotes entire populations of Scandinavia and their settlements from the late 8th to the 11th century. 3. They had two distinct classes of ships: the longship and the knarr.
THE MOORS	**CHRÉTIEN DE TROYES**
1. The most important influence brought about by their occupation was the use of Arabic numerals, which we still use today. 2. They brought new words to Europe. Examples are *algebra, lute, magazine, orange* and *tariff.* 3. They introduced the game of chess.	1. This 12th-century writer recounted the tales of King Arthur. 2. Some of his Arthurian tales included the wizard Merlin. 3. His tales of Arthur included the Knights of the Round Table (Lancelot, Gawain, Galahad, and others).
THE BLACK DEATH	**KING ARTHUR**
1. The term refers to the bubonic plague. 2. It caused the death of 25 million people between 1347 and 1352. 3. In the early 1330s an outbreak of this deadly disease occurred in China. It spread to western Asia and to Europe because of trade.	1. He is an important figure in the mythology of Great Britain and the central character in popular legends. 2. There is disagreement about whether this legendary figure ever actually existed. 3. In later versions of the stories, he gathered the Knights of the Round Table and held court at Camelot.

TOURNAMENTS 1. These military exercises not only entertained the nobility, but also kept the knights prepared for battle. 2. Early ones were mock battles called melees. 3. In later years the jousters who took part in these were separated from each other by a barrier called a tilt.	**HERALDIC DEVICES** 1. One reason for their growing use was the desire to distinguish between contestants in tournaments. 2. The science of reading these was called blazonry. 3. Coats of arms are these.
THE CHURCH 1. Because of its importance, the Middle Ages is often called the Golden Age of Faith. 2. During the high Middle Ages, it became organized into an elaborate hierarchy with the pope as the head in western Europe. 3. It collected a tithe from the tenants on the lord's manor and received a plot of land called a glebe.	**TRIAL BY ORDEAL** 1. Divination, physical and combat were three types. 2. Its use was based on the belief that the outcome would reflect the judgment of God. 3. Until the thirteenth century when it was condemned by the Church, it was a method of determining guilt or innocence.
THE CRUSADES 1. They were religious wars fought by Christians to gain back what they considered the Holy Land from the Muslims. 2. The Third was led by Richard I, known as Richard the Lionheart. 3. Pope Urban II recruited men to fight these wars.	**MONKS** 1. Most followed the rules established by Benedict of Nursia in 529. 2. The rules they followed covered every hour of every day. 3. The Hospitallers and the Templars were two orders.
MERCHANTS 1. No matter what they bought or sold, those in the same town belonged to the same guild. 2. This class rose because of the growth of towns and the increase in trade. 3. Along with the craftsmen, they formed guilds to protect their interests.	**CRAFTSMEN** 1. Their guilds served two purposes: to protect the members and to insure the high quality of the goods they made. 2. They had three stages of training: apprentice, journeyman and master. 3. They could only open their own shop and train apprentices if the members of his guild declared their work a masterpiece.
FAIRS 1. They were more than a marketplace; jugglers, musicians and other amusements were also included. 2. Townspeople set up booths on the public square to entice traveling merchants to their town. 3. In later years the places and times of the year when they were held were fixed. The Middle Ages Bingo	**GEOFFREY CHAUCER** 1. He wrote the *Canterbury Tales*. 2. His tales were written from the point of view of pilgrims traveling to Canterbury. 3. Among the characters in his tales were a knight, a prioress, a monk, a friar and a miller. © Barbara M. Peller

RICHARD I 1. He was often referred to as Richard the Lionheart, Coeur de Lion. 2. He was King of England from 1189 to 1199 and was considered a hero. 3. He fought in the Third Crusade.	**CHARLEMAGNE** 1. He became king of the Franks in 768. 2. In 800 Pope Leo III crowned this Frank king emperor. 3. When he was crowned emperor in 800, the Western Roman Empire was restored.
CHANSONS DE GESTE 1. These French epic poems combined historic fact and legend. 2. These epic poems dealt with the exploits of Charlemagne and his followers. 3. A famous one was Chanson de Roland.	**THE FEUDAL SYSTEM** 1. It is a social system based on mutual obligations between lord and vassal. 2. Under this system a fief, or estate, was granted by the lord to his vassal. 3. Under this system the vassal formally surrendered to the lord in a ceremony called homage.
BATTLE OF HASTINGS 1. The leaders of this battle were William of Normandy and Harold, Earl of Essex. 2. It took place on October 14, 1066. 3. The Bayeaux Tapestry depicted this and other events that led to the Norman conquest of England.	**WILLIAM THE CONQUEROR** 1. He was crowned king of England a few weeks after defeating Harold at Hastings. 2. He ordered an elaborate survey of England; it became known as the *Domesday Book.* 3. He and Harold fought over succession to the throne when Edward the Confessor died in 1066.
THE DARK AGES 1. This term is sometimes used to refer to Europe in the Early Middle Ages. 2. Today historians use the term to express the scarcity of historical records and artistic and cultural output compared to later times. 3. The term was first used by the Italian scholar Petrarch in the 1330s to describe the period beginning in the late fifth century.	**CASTLE** 1. A motte and bailey was one type. 2. A moat surrounded it. 3. A heavy timber or metal grill, called a portcullis, protected its entrance and could be raised or lowered from within it.
KNIGHTS 1. They had to go through the stages of page, squire and armiger. 2. Not all squires became this, but those who did officially became one during a ceremony that included an oath of loyalty. 3. Their most important weapon was a lance.	**SUITS OF ARMOR** 1. Until the fourteenth century most were chain mail. 2. When the longbows came into use in the fourteenth century, more protection was needed and it became heavier and thicker. 3. Gauntlets were the protective gloves worn with them.

The Middle Ages Bingo

THE MAGNA CARTA
1. It was signed and sealed on June 15, 1215.
2. The barons rebelled against the King of England and demanded liberties; these liberties were enumerated in this document.
3. It granted rights to both barons and their vassals and included the right to trial by a jury of one's peers.

FERDINAND MAGELLAN
1. This Renaissance explorer was born in Portugal in 1480.
2. In 1519 he sailed around the tip of South America. The strait he found was named for him.
3. He found a new ocean and named it the Pacific.

THOMAS À BECKET
1. He was appointed Archbishop of Canterbury by King Henry II in 1162.
2. He and King Henry quarreled and Henry's knights killed him in the Canterbury Cathedral in 1170.
3. He was canonized (declared to be a saint) in 1173.

EL CID
1. This great military leader and the national hero of Spain lived from c.1044 to 1099.
2. His real name was Rodrigo Díaz de Vivar (or Ruy Díaz de Vivar) and he was also known as El Campeador, or "The Champion."
3. After his death this Spanish hero became the subject of many legends, stories, and poems, including a 12th-century epic.

CHIVALRY
1. It's the generic term for the virtues & qualities the knightly system inspired in its followers.
2. Its conventions directed men to honor, serve, and do nothing to displease ladies and maidens.
3. The term evolved from words such as chevalier (French), caballero (Spanish), and cavaliere (Italian), all meaning "a warrior who fights on horseback."

ST. FRANCIS OF ASSISI
1. In 1209 he founded the Franciscan Order of friars.
2. The son of a prosperous businessman, he gave up all his worldly goods and set out to preach repentance. He was very influential in thirteenth-century Church reform.
3. With Saint Clare he founded the Order of Poor Clares.

MARCO POLO
1. In 1271, he left Venice with his father and uncle on a eastward trek and in 1275 met Kublai Khan, also known as the Great Khan.
2. Kublai Khan conscripted him into service for the Mongol Empire.
3. He wrote a book of his travels; it was widely published although many of his accounts are thought to be greatly exaggerated.

SALADIN
1. During the Third Crusade, he managed to keep the greatest fighters from the West from making any significant advances, including Richard the Lionheart.
2. He recaptured Jerusalem from the Crusaders.
3. In 1192, he and Richard signed the Treaty of Ramia; he agreed to let Christians continue to make pilgrimages to Jerusalem.

POPE URBAN II
1. He developed most of the reforms of Gregory VII and helped turn the papacy into a strong political entity.
2. He made a speech calling for all Christian knights to take back the Holy Land from the Turks, thus launching the First Crusade.
3. His speech at the Council of Clermont in 1095 instigated the Crusades.

CATHEDRALS
1. They were larger than castles, symbolizing their importance to medieval society where religion dominated everyone's life.
2. Many had beautiful stained glass windows that retold stories from the Bible.
3. Canterbury and York were each the site of an important one.

CHRISTOPHER COLUMBUS
1. This Renaissance explorer was born in Genoa, Italy, in 1451.
2. He was granted three ships for his first voyage: the *Pinta,* the *Santa Maria,* and the *Niña.*
3. He landed in the New World on October 12, 1492.

THE RENAISSANCE
1. The name of this cultural movement means "rebirth."
2. It began in Italy in the late Middle Ages and later spread to the rest of western Europe.
3. This period saw developments in most intellectual pursuits, but is best known for its developments in art.

JOAN OF ARC
1. This simple peasant girl claimed to hear the voices of saints telling her to help the Dauphin gain the throne of France.
2. She was captured, tried and burned by the English as a heretic in 1431.
3. Her martyrdom united the French, who drove the English out of France 20 years later.

GOTHIC ARCHITECTURE
1. Its characteristic features include the pointed arch, the ribbed vault and the flying buttress.
2. It was the style of many European cathedrals, abbeys, churches and other buildings during the high and late medieval period.
3. This term first appeared during the late Renaissance as an insult. During the period in which it *flourished,* it was called the French style.

JOHANNES GUTENBERG
1. In 1440, this German inventor invented a printing-press process that remained the main means of printing until the late 20th century.
2. His method of printing from movable type led to the mass production of printed books.
3. His invention involved a machine that transferred lettering or images by contact with various forms of inked surface onto paper.

MICHELANGELO
1. This Renaissance artist is famous for the painting of the scenes from *Genesis* on the ceiling of the Sistine Chapel.
2. Two of his best-known works, the *Pietà* and the *David,* were sculpted before he turned thirty.
3. It took him approximately four years to complete the painting of the ceiling of the Sistine Chapel: 1508–1512.

ELEANOR OF AQUITAINE
1. She was one of the wealthiest and most powerful women in Europe during the High Middle Ages.
2. She was the mother of two kings of England, Richard I and John.
3. She is known for her participation in the Second Crusade.

LEONARDO DA VINCI
1. Often described as the archetype of the "Renaissance man," he was a mathematician, scientist, engineer, inventor, anatomist, painter, sculptor, architect, botanist, musician and writer.
2. His best known works are the *Mona Lisa* and *The Last Supper.*
3. His *Mona Lisa* and *The Last Supper* are said to be the most reproduced paintings of all time.

COPERNICUS
1. This Polish astronomer was first to formulate a scientifically based cosmology that said Earth was not the center of the universe.
2. This Polish astronomer said that the spheres revolve about the sun as their mid-point, and therefore the sun is the center of the universe.
3. The heliocentric ideas of this Polish astronomer were rejected by the Catholic Church.

FABLES
1. These tales, designed to teach a lesson about conduct by giving an example of behavior, became popular during the Middle Ages.
2. Many of these anthropomorphic tales featured animals with human feelings and emotions.
3. Among the best known are the 12-century satirical tales that originated in France, *Roman de Renart,* featuring Renart the Fox.

The Middle Ages Bingo

The Middle Ages Bingo

Battle of Hastings	Charlemagne	Castle	Peasants	William the Conqueror
The Church	Tournaments	Heraldic Devices	The Feudal System	Merchants
Craftsmen	Chanson de Geste		Knights	Suits of Armor
The Black Death	Chivalry	The Renaissance	Fairs	Richard I
Geoffrey Chaucer	The Vikings	The Magna Carta	Trial by Ordeal	Ferdinand Magellan

The Middle Ages Bingo

The Middle Ages	Chartres	The Moors	Peasants	King Arthur
Dante Alighieri	Fables	Marco Polo	The Magna Carta	Copernicus
Monks	Leif Erikson		Craftsmen	William the Conqueror
The Vikings	Michelangelo	Fairs	Cathedrals	Knights
Thomas à Becket	Castles	Gothic Architecture	The Crusades	Leonardo da Vinci

The Middle Ages Bingo

Marco Polo	Eleanor of Aquitaine	Fairs	Saladin	Christopher Columbus
St. Francis of Assisi	Merchants	Chivalry	The Renaissance	El Cid
Thomas à Becket	The Dark Ages		Monks	Pope Urban II
Joan of Arc	Charlemagne	King Arthur	Cathedrals	The Crusades
The Magna Carta	Leif Erikson	Ferdinand Magellan	The Black Death	Leonardo da Vinci

The Middle Ages Bingo

Gothic Architecture	Chartres	The Feudal System	Chivalry	Craftsmen
Trial by Ordeal	Michelangelo	Dante Alighieri	The Renaissance	Monks
Copernicus	Leonardo da Vinci		Knights	St. Francis of Assisi
The Moors	Joan of Arc	Marco Polo	Cathedrals	Fables
Johannes Gutenberg	Merchants	The Black Death	King Arthur	Saladin

The Middle Ages Bingo

Fables	Copernicus	The Middle Ages	Fairs	Peasants
The Crusades	Monks	Chrétien de Troyes	Trial by Ordeal	William the Conqueror
Richard I	The Feudal System		Merchants	Suits of Armor
Gothic Architecture	Pope Urban II	The Church	Geoffrey Chaucer	Knights
Heraldic Devices	Castles	Joan of Arc	The Vikings	Cathedrals

The Middle Ages Bingo

The Middle Ages	Fairs	Joan of Arc	William the Conqueror	Leif Erikson
Copernicus	The Church	Johannes Gutenberg	St. Francis of Assisi	Eleanor of Aquitaine
Tournaments	Marco Polo		Saladin	Chartres
The Dark Ages	Fables	Battle of Hastings	The Moors	Christopher Columbus
Castles	El Cid	Dante Alighieri	Chivalry	The Black Death

The Middle Ages Bingo: Card No. 6

The Middle Ages Bingo

Pope Urban II	Cathedrals	Peasants	Joan of Arc	Heraldic Devices
Chansons de Geste	Knights	The Magna Carta	Ferdinand Magellan	Richard I
Gothic Architecture	Leonardo da Vinci		Craftsmen	Monks
Chivalry	Michelangelo	The Black Death	The Crusades	Merchants
The Feudal System	Geoffrey Chaucer	King Arthur	William the Conqueror	Chrétien de Troyes

The Middle Ages Bingo

Peasants	Cathedrals	Michelangelo	Chartres	The Magna Carta
Merchants	Chansons de Geste	The Dark Ages	Charlemagne	Johannes Gutenberg
Craftsmen	The Middle Ages		The Church	Tournaments
Marco Polo	The Feudal System	Fairs	Castles	Richard I
King Arthur	Christopher Columbus	Battle of Hastings	Fables	The Renaissance

The Middle Ages Bingo

Chivalry	Castles	Craftsmen	Fairs	King Arthur
The Black Death	Michelangelo	Thomas à Becket	Leonardo da Vinci	Suits of Armor
The Vikings	Peasants		The Church	Gothic Architecture
Fables	William the Conqueror	Christopher Columbus	Monks	Knights
Dante Alighieri	Merchants	Joan of Arc	Ferdinand Magellan	The Moors

The Middle Ages Bingo

Marco Polo	Knights	Merchants	Chansons de Geste	William the Conqueror
Joan of Arc	Geoffrey Chaucer	Fairs	The Magna Carta	Tournaments
Cathedrals	Chrétien de Troyes		Trial by Ordeal	Ferdinand Magellan
The Feudal System	The Church	Monks	Battle of Hastings	Saladin
The Moors	Craftsmen	Richard I	Peasants	The Renaissance

The Middle Ages Bingo

The Middle Ages	Fairs	The Feudal System	The Dark Ages	Michelangelo
King Arthur	William the Conqueror	Thomas à Becket	El Cid	Craftsmen
Saladin	Eleanor of Aquitaine		Chartres	Christopher Columbus
Joan of Arc	The Crusades	Cathedrals	Monks	Pope Urban II
Knights	The Renaissance	Leif Erikson	Charlemagne	Chivalry

The Middle Ages Bingo

St. Francis of Assisi	Knights	Castles	Peasants	Gothic Architecture
The Magna Carta	Fables	Richard I	Johannes Gutenberg	Heraldic Devices
Michelangelo	The Church		Craftsmen	Battle of Hastings
Trial by Ordeal	El Cid	The Vikings	Merchants	Copernicus
Leonardo da Vinci	Suits of Armor	The Crusades	The Renaissance	Leif Erikson

The Middle Ages Bingo

Geoffrey Chaucer	Trial by Ordeal	Tournaments	Fables	Leif Erikson
The Church	Ferdinand Magellan	The Middle Ages	Castles	Merchants
Monks	Chartres		Craftsmen	Peasants
Pope Urban II	Knights	Chrétien de Troyes	The Crusades	Copernicus
Marco Polo	The Feudal System	The Moors	William the Conqueror	The Renaissance

The Middle Ages Bingo: Card No. 13

The Middle Ages Bingo

Suits of Armor	Chartres	The Feudal System	Gothic Architecture	The Middle Ages
Geoffrey Chaucer	Michelangelo	Fables	Heraldic Devices	El Cid
The Black Death	The Renaissance		The Church	Leonardo da Vinci
Battle of Hastings	Copernicus	Peasants	King Arthur	Knights
The Vikings	Craftsmen	Monks	Merchants	William the Conqueror

The Middle Ages Bingo

Joan of Arc	Marco Polo	Richard I	William the Conqueror	Copernicus
The Renaissance	Fables	Thomas à Becket	St. Francis of Assisi	Peasants
Fairs	Leonardo da Vinci		Tournaments	Trial by Ordeal
Chivalry	Heraldic Devices	Dante Alighieri	Merchants	Craftsmen
Chansons de Geste	The Black Death	Battle of Hastings	Knights	Chrétien de Troyes

The Middle Ages Bingo

The Magna Carta	Chartres	Charlemagne	Michelangelo	Gothic Architecture
Heraldic Devices	Cathedrals	Suits of Armor	Leonardo da Vinci	Copernicus
Chivalry	Eleanor of Aquitaine		Monks	Geoffrey Chaucer
The Middle Ages	Chansons de Geste	Knights	Castles	Peasants
The Moors	The Renaissance	The Church	Merchants	Battle of Hastings

The Middle Ages Bingo

Tournaments	Chartres	The Black Death	Fairs	Trial by Ordeal
The Church	Craftsmen	Chivalry	Heraldic Devices	William the Conqueror
Charlemagne	King Arthur		Chrétien de Troyes	Monks
The Feudal System	Peasants	Gothic Architecture	Geoffrey Chaucer	Merchants
Suits of Armor	Battle of Hastings	Pope Urban II	Chansons de Geste	Knights

The Middle Ages Bingo

El Cid	Knights	Craftsmen	The Renaissance	The Dark Ages
Christopher Columbus	Trial by Ordeal	Peasants	The Church	Marco Polo
Gothic Architecture	Merchants		The Black Death	Copernicus
The Crusades	Heraldic Devices	The Feudal System	Monks	Geoffrey Chaucer
William the Conqueror	Tournaments	The Moors	Charlemagne	Battle of Hastings

The Middle Ages Bingo

The Middle Ages	Ferdinand Magellan	Chansons de Geste	The Magna Carta	Chivalry
Peasants	Knights	Michelangelo	Battle of Hastings	Castles
Tournaments	Johannes Gutenberg		Eleanor of Aquitaine	The Black Death
The Renaissance	William the Conqueror	Gothic Architecture	Merchants	Leif Erikson
Leonardo da Vinci	Pope Urban II	Cathedrals	The Feudal System	King Arthur

The Middle Ages Bingo

The Magna Carta	Knights	Chansons de Geste	Heraldic Devices	Richard I
Gothic Architecture	Johannes Gutenberg	Peasants	Suits of Armor	Cathedrals
Eleanor of Aquitaine	The Black Death		Monks	The Middle Ages
Fairs	Geoffrey Chaucer	The Feudal System	Merchants	Battle of Hastings
The Church	Chrétien de Troyes	Fables	The Crusades	Trial by Ordeal

The Middle Ages Bingo

Battle of Hastings	Chartres	Chivalry	Castles	The Renaissance
Heraldic Devices	Richard I	Saladin	Michelangelo	William the Conqueror
Gothic Architecture	Charlemagne		Merchants	Peasants
Monks	The Black Death	The Church	Chansons de Geste	Trial by Ordeal
The Feudal System	The Middle Ages	Geoffrey Chaucer	The Crusades	The Magna Carta

The Middle Ages Bingo

Monks	Chartres	Castles	Fairs	Chivalry
St. Francis of Assisi	Richard I	Battle of Hastings	Tournaments	Gothic Architecture
Heraldic Devices	The Middle Ages		Merchants	Charlemagne
The Vikings	The Renaissance	The Black Death	Chrétien de Troyes	Fables
The Magna Carta	Chansons de Geste	The Crusades	Pope Urban II	William the Conqueror

The Middle Ages Bingo

The Black Death	Chartres	Monks	Richard I	Joan of Arc
The Crusades	Copernicus	Heraldic Devices	St. Francis of Assisi	Leonardo da Vinci
The Church	The Renaissance		Knights	Gothic Architecture
Geoffrey Chaucer	Peasants	Merchants	Christopher Columbus	William the Conqueror
The Vikings	Craftsmen	Pope Urban II	The Moors	Cathedrals

The Middle Ages Bingo

Chansons de Geste	Richard I	Peasants	Castles	The Magna Carta
The Feudal System	Joan of Arc	The Crusades	Marco Polo	William the Conqueror
Chartres	Battle of Hastings		The Black Death	Fables
Tournaments	Heraldic Devices	Chrétien de Troyes	Copernicus	Geoffrey Chaucer
Leif Erikson	Charlemagne	Gothic Architecture	Merchants	El Cid

© Barbara M. Peller

The Middle Ages Bingo

The Renaissance	The Middle Ages	Castles	The Dark Ages	Suits of Armor
The Feudal System	Monks	Richard I	St. Francis of Assisi	Saladin
El Cid	Battle of Hastings		Chansons de Geste	Heraldic Devices
Charlemagne	Peasants	The Black Death	Gothic Architecture	Knights
Fables	Geoffrey Chaucer	Merchants	Craftsmen	William the Conqueror

The Middle Ages Bingo: Card No. 25

The Middle Ages Bingo

St. Francis of Assisi	Ferdinand Magellan	Knights	William the Conqueror	The Magna Carta
The Renaissance	Fables	El Cid	Marco Polo	Craftsmen
Chansons de Geste	King Arthur		Christopher Columbus	Suits of Armor
The Black Death	Geoffrey Chaucer	Gothic Architecture	Chrétien de Troyes	Charlemagne
Johannes Gutenberg	Heraldic Devices	Saladin	Battle of Hastings	Castles

The Middle Ages Bingo

Johannes Gutenberg	Thomas à Becket	Peasants	Fairs	The Feudal System
Gothic Architecture	Heraldic Devices	Chivalry	Eleanor of Aquitaine	Tournaments
Chansons de Geste	Knights		Charlemagne	Battle of Hastings
Monks	The Crusades	The Black Death	Fables	Geoffrey Chaucer
Merchants	Copernicus	William the Conqueror	Pope Urban II	The Moors

The Middle Ages Bingo

The Feudal System	Richard I	Chansons de Geste	Chivalry	William the Conqueror
Battle of Hastings	Castles	Monks	Chrétien de Troyes	Trial by Ordeal
The Middle Ages	The Renaissance		Geoffrey Chaucer	Fairs
Heraldic Devices	Fables	The Crusades	Eleanor of Aquitaine	Charlemagne
Gothic Architecture	Leif Erikson	Merchants	Knights	The Black Death

The Middle Ages Bingo

King Arthur	Chivalry	Richard I	William the Conqueror	Gothic Architecture
Dante Alighieri	Chartres	Cathedrals	Johannes Gutenberg	Tournaments
Pope Urban II	Heraldic Devices		The Vikings	Charlemagne
Chansons de Geste	Saladin	Merchants	Fables	The Crusades
The Feudal System	Knights	The Black Death	Castles	Monks

The Middle Ages Bingo

Thomas à Becket	Chansons de Geste	Geoffrey Chaucer	The Dark Ages	Tournaments
The Feudal System	Merchants	Battle of Hastings	St. Francis of Assisi	El Cid
Peasants	Chivalry		Ferdinand Magellan	Trial by Ordeal
Heraldic Devices	Pope Urban II	Knights	Castles	Michelangelo
The Church	Craftsmen	Joan of Arc	William the Conqueror	Charlemagne